# De-Identification of Personally Identifiable Information

U.S. Department of Commerce

i

## Reports on Computer Systems Technology

The Information Technology Laboratory (ITL) at the National Institute of Standards and Technology (NIST) promotes the U.S. economy and public welfare by providing technical leadership for the Nation's measurement and standards infrastructure. ITL develops tests, test methods, reference data, proof of concept implementations, and technical analyses to advance the development and productive use of information technology. ITL's responsibilities include the development of management, administrative, technical, and physical standards and guidelines for the cost-effective security and privacy of other than national security-related information in Federal information systems.

## Abstract

De-identification is the removal of identifying information from data. Several US laws, regulations and policies specify that data should be de-identified prior to sharing as a control to protect the privacy of the data subjects. In recent years researchers have shown that some de-identified data can sometimes be re-identified. This document summarizes roughly two decades of de-identification research, discusses current practices, and presents opportunities for future research.

## Keywords

De-identification; HIPAA Privacy Rule; k-anonymity; re-identification; privacy

## Acknowledgements

We wish to thank Khaled El Emam, Bradley Malin, Latanya Sweeney and Christine M. Task for answering questions and reviewing earlier versions of this document.

## Audience

This document is intended for use by officials, advocacy groups and other members of the community that are concerned with the policy issues involving the creation, use and sharing of data sets containing personally identifiable information. It is also designed to provide technologists and researchers with an overview of the technical issues in the de-identification of data sets. While this document assumes a high-level understanding of information system security technologies, it is intended to be accessible to a wide audience. For this reason, this document minimizes the use of mathematical notation.

## Note to Reviewers

NIST requests comments especially on the following:

- Is the terminology that is provided consistent with current usage?
- To what extent should this document's subject be broadened to discuss differential privacy and statistical disclosure limitation techniques?
- Should the glossary be expanded? If so, please suggest words, definitions, and appropriate citations.

**Table of Contents**

135

# 1   Introduction

Government agencies, businesses and other organizations are increasingly under pressure to make raw data available to outsiders. When collected data contain personally identifiable information (PII) such as names or Social Security numbers (SSNs), there can be a conflict between the goals of sharing data and protecting privacy. *De-identification* is one way that organizations can balance these competing goals.

De-identification is a process by which a data custodian alters or removes identifying information from a data set, making it harder for users of the data to determine the identities of the data subjects. Once de-identified, data can be shared with trusted parties that are bound by data use agreements that only allow specific uses. In this case, de-identification makes it easier for trusted parties to comply with privacy requirements. Alternatively, the de-identified data can be distributed with fewer controls to a broader audience. In this case, de-identification is a tool designed to assist privacy-preserving data publishing (PPDP).

De-identification is not without risk. There are many de-identification techniques with differing levels of effectiveness. In general, privacy protection improves as more aggressive de-identification techniques are employed, but less utility remains in the resulting data set. As long as any utility remains in the data, there exists the possibility that some information might be linked back to the original identities, a process called *re-identification*. The use of de-identified data can also result in other harms to the data subjects, even without having the data first re-identified.

## 1.1   Document Purpose and Scope

This document provides an overview of de-identification issues and terminology. It summarizes significant publications to date involving de-identification and re-identification.

## 1.2   Intended Audience

This document is intended for use by officials, advocacy groups and other members of the community that are concerned with the policy issues involving the creation, use and sharing of data sets containing personally identifiable information. It is also designed to provide technologists and researchers with an overview of the technical issues in the de-identification of data sets. While this document assumes a high-level understanding of information system security technologies, it is intended to be accessible to a wide audience. For this reason, this document minimizes the use of mathematical notation.

## 1.3   Organization

The remainder of this report is organized as follows: Section 2 introduces the concepts of de-identification, re-identification and data sharing models. Section 3 discusses *syntactic de-identification*, a class of de-identification techniques that rely on the masking or altering of fields in tabular data. Section 4 discusses current challenges of de-identification information that are not tabular data, such as free-format text, images, and genomic information. Section 5 concludes. Appendix A is a glossary, and Appendix B provides a list of additional resources.

174 ## 2   De-identification, Re-Identification, and Data Sharing Models

175   This section explains the motivation for de-identification, discusses the use of re-identification
176   attacks to gauge the effectiveness of de-identification, and describes models for sharing de-
177   identified data. It also introduces the terminology used in this report.

178   ### 2.1   Motivation
179   Increasingly organizations that are collecting data and maintaining databases are under
180   challenged to protect the data while using and sharing as widely as possible. For government
181   databases, data sharing can increase transparency, provide new resources to private industry, and
182   lead to more efficient government as a whole. Private firms can also benefit from data sharing in
183   the form of increased publicity, civic engagement, and potentially increased revenue if the data
184   are sold.

185   When datasets contains personally identifiable information such as names, email addresses,
186   geolocation information, or photographs, there can be a conflict between the goals of effective
187   data use and privacy protection. Many data sharing exercises appear to violate the Fair
188   Information Practice Principles[1] of **Purpose Specification**[2] and **Use Limitation**[3]. Retaining a
189   database of personal information after it is no longer needed, because it was expensive to create
190   and the data might be useful in the future, may be a violation of the **Data Minimization**[4]
191   principle.

192   De-identification represents an attempt to uphold the privacy promise of the FIPPs while
193   allowing for data re-use, with the justification that the individuals' will not suffer a harm from
194   the use of their data because their identifying information has been removed from the dataset.

195   Several US laws and regulations specifically recognize the importance and utility of data de-
196   identification:

197   - The Department of Education has held that the Family and Educational Records Privacy
198     Act does not apply to de-identified student records. "Educational agencies and
199     institutions are permitted to release, without consent, educational records, or information
200     from educational records that have been de-identified through the removal of all
201     personally identifiable information."[5]

---

[1] National Strategy for Trusted Identities in Cyberspace, Appendix A—Fair Information Practice Principles. April 15, 2011.
http://www.nist.gov/nstic/NSTIC-FIPPs.pdf

[2] "**Purpose Specification:** Organizations should specifically articulate the authority that permits the collection of PII and specifically articulate the purpose or purposes for which the PII is intended to be used." Ibid.

[3] "**Use Limitation:** Organizations should use PII solely for the purpose(s) specified in the notice. Sharing PII should be for a purpose compatible with the purpose for which the PII was collected." Ibid.

[4] "**Data Minimization:** Organizations should only collect PII that is directly relevant and necessary to accomplish the specified purpose(s) and only retain PII for as long as is necessary to fulfill the specified purpose(s)."

[5] Dear Colleague Letter about Family Educational Rights and Privacy Act (FERPA) Final Regulations, US Department of Education, December 17, 2008. http://www2.ed.gov/policy/gen/guid/fpco/hottopics/ht12-17-08 html

202
203
204
205

- The Health Insurance Portability and Accountability Act (HIPAA) Privacy Rule allows de-identified medical records to be used without any restriction, provided that organizations distributing the records have no direct knowledge that the records can be re-identified.[6]

206
207
208

- The Health Information Technology for Economic and Clinical Health Act (HITECH Act) requirements for security and privacy explicitly do not apply to the "use, disclosure, or request of protected health information that has been de-identified."[7]

209
210

- The Foodborne illness surveillance system is required to allow "timely public access to aggregated, de-identified surveillance data."[8]

211
212

- Entities contracted by Health and Human Services to provide drug safety data must have the ability to provide that data in de-identified form.[9]

213
214

- Voluntary safety reports submitted to the Federal Aviation Submission are not protected from public disclosure if the data that they contain is de-identified.[10]

215
216
217
218

Each of these laws and regulations implicitly assume that it is possible to remove personally identifiable information from a data set in a way that protects privacy but still leaves useful information. They also assume that de-identified information will not be re-identified at a later point in time.

219
220
221
222
223
224

In practice many de-identification techniques are not able to provide such strong privacy guarantees. Section 3.2 and Section 3.5 discuss some of the well-publicized cases in which data that were thought to be properly de-identified were published and then later re-identified by researchers or journalists. The results of these re-identifications violated the privacy of the data subjects, who were not previously identified as being in the dataset. Additional privacy harms can result from the disclosure of specific attributes that the data set linked to the identities.

225

## 2.2   Models for Privacy-Preserving use of Private Information

226
227

Academics have identified two distinct models for making use of personally identifiable information in a database while protecting the privacy of the data subjects:

228
229
230

- ***Privacy Preserving Data Mining.*** In this model, data are not released, but are used instead for statistical processing or machine learning. The results of the calculations may be released in the form of statistical tables, classifiers, or other kinds of results.

---

[6] 45 CFR 160, 45 CFR 162, and 45 CFR 164. See also "Combined Regulation Text of All Rules," US Department of Health and Human Services, Office for Civil Rights, Health Information Privacy.
http://www.hhs.gov/ocr/privacy/hipaa/administrative/combined/index.html

[7] 42 USC 17935

[8] 21 USC 2224

[9] 21 USC 355

[10] 49 USC 44735

231      •    ***Privacy Preserving Data Publishing.*** In this model, data are processed to produce a new
232           data product that is distributed to users.

233 Privacy Preserving Data Mining (PPDM) is a broad term for any use of sensitive information to
234 publish public statistics. Statistical reports that summarize confidential survey data are an
235 example of PPDM.

236 ***Statistical Disclosure Limitation***[11] is a set of principles and techniques that have been developed
237 by researchers concerned with the generation and publication of official statistics. The goal of
238 disclosure limitation is to prevent published statistics from impacting the privacy of those
239 surveyed. Techniques developed for disclosure limitation include generalization of reported
240 information to broader categories, swapping data between similar entities, and the addition of
241 noise in reports.

242 ***Differential Privacy*** is a set of techniques based on a mathematical definition of privacy and
243 information leakage from operations on a data set by the introduction of non-deterministic
244 noise.[12] Differential privacy holds that the results of a data analysis should be roughly the same
245 before and after the addition or removal of a single data record (which is usually taken to be the
246 data from a single individual). In its basic form differential privacy is applied to online query
247 systems, but differential privacy can also be used to produce machine-learning statistical
248 classifiers and synthetic data sets.[13]

249 Differential privacy is an active research area, but to date there have been few applications of
250 differential privacy techniques to actual running systems. Two notable exceptions are the Census
251 Bureau's "OnTheMap" website, which uses differential privacy to create reasonably accurate
252 block-level synthetic census data;[14] and Fredrikson et al.'s study to determine the impact of
253 applying differential privacy to a clinical trial that created a statistical model for correlating
254 genomic information and warfarin dosage.[15] The Fredrikson study concluded that the models
255 constructed using differential privacy gains came at the cost of would result negative clinical
256 outcomes for a significant number of patients.

257 Privacy Preserving Data Publishing (PPDP) allows for information based on private data to be
258 published, allowing other researchers to perform novel analyses. The goal of PPDP is to provide

---

[11] Statistical Policy Working Paper 22 (Second version, 2005), Report on Statistical Disclosure Limitation Methodology, Federal Committee on Statistical Methodology, December 2005.

[12] Cynthia Dwork, Differential Privacy, in ICALP, Springer, 2006

[13] Marco Gaboardi, Emilio Jesús Gallego Arias, Justin Hsu, Aaron, Zhiwei Steven Wu, Dual Query: Practical Private Query Release for High Dimensional Data, Proceedings of the 31st Intenrational Conference on Machine Learning, Beijing, China. 2014. JMLR: W&CP volume 32.

[14] Abowd et al., "Formal Privacy Guarantees and Analytical Validity of OnTheMap Public-use Data," Joint NSF-Census-IRS Workshop on Synthetic Data and Confidentiality Protection, Suitland, MD, July 31, 2009.

[15] Fredrikson et al., Privacy in Pharmacogenetics: An End-to-End Case Study of Personalized Wafrin Dosing, 23rd Usenix Security Symposium, August 20-22, 2014, San Diego, CA.

259    data that have high utility without compromising the privacy of the data subjects.

260    ***De-identification*** is the "general term for any process of removing the association between a set
261    of identifying data and the data subject." (ISO/TS 25237-2008) De-identification is designed to
262    protect individual privacy while preserving some of the dataset's utility for other purposes. De-
263    identification protects the privacy of individuals, making it hard or impossible to learn if an
264    individual's data is in a data set, or to determine any attributes about an individual known to be
265    in the data set. De-identification is one of the primary tools for achieving PPDP.

266    ***Synthetic data generation*** uses some PPDM techniques to create a dataset that is similar to the
267    original data, but where some or all of the resulting data elements are generated and do not map
268    to actual individuals. As such synthetic data generation can be seen as a fusion of PPDM and
269    PPDP.

270    **2.3   De-Identification Data Flow Model**

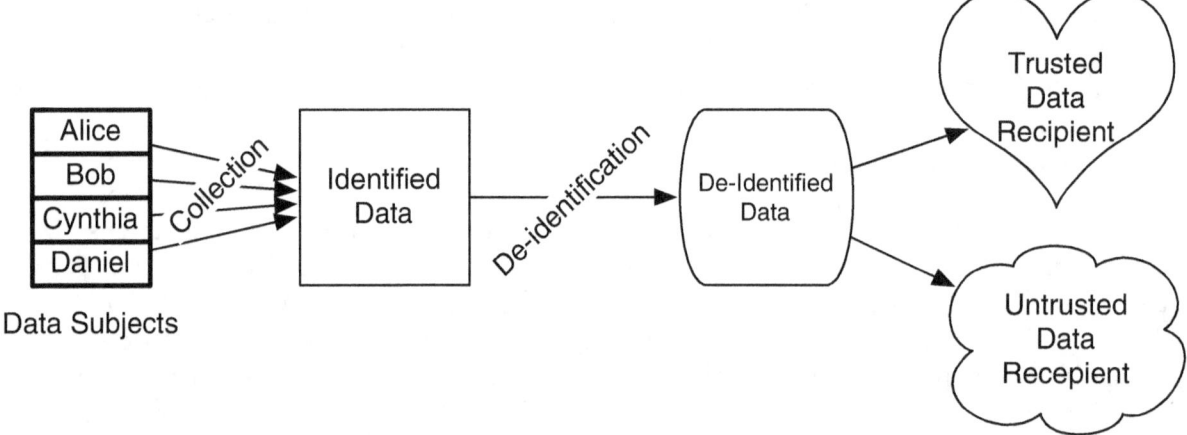

271
272                          **Figure 1: Data Collection, De-Identification and Use**

273    Figure 1 provides an overview of the de-identification process. Data are collected from ***Data***
274    ***Subjects,*** the "persons to whom data refer." (ISO/TS 25237-2008) These data are combined into
275    a ***data set*** containing *personally identifiable information* (PII). De-identification creates a new
276    data set of *de-identified data.* This data set may eventually be used by a small number of trusted
277    data recipients. Alternatively, the data might be made broadly available to a larger (potentially
278    limitless) number of untrusted data recipients.

279    ***Pseudonymization*** is a specific kind of de-identification in which the direct identifiers are
280    replaced with pseudonyms (ISO/TS 25237:2008). If the pseudonymization follows a repeatable
281    algorithm, different practitioners can match records belonging to the same individual from
282    different data sets. However, the same practitioners will have the ability to re-identify the
283    pseudonymized data as part of the matching process. Pseudonymization can also be reversed if
284    the entity that performed the pseudonymization retains a table linking the original identities to
285    the pseudonyms, a technique called *unmasking.*

286    **2.4   Re-identification Risk and Data Utility**
287    Those receiving de-identified data may attempt to learn the identities of the data subjects that

288  have been removed. This process is called *re-identification*. Because an important goal of de-
289  identification is to prevent unauthorized re-identification, such attempts are sometimes called *re-*
290  *identification attacks.*

291  The term "attack" is borrowed from the literature of computer security, in which the security of a
292  computer system or encryption algorithm is analyzed through the use of a hypothetical "attacker"
293  in possession of specific skills, knowledge, and access. A risk assessment involves cataloging the
294  range of potential attackers and, for each, the likelihood of success.

295  There are many reasons that an individual or organization might attempt a re-identification
296  attack:

297  - **To test the quality of the de-identification.** For example, a researcher might conduct the
298    re-identification attack at the request of the data custodian performing the de-
299    identification
300  - **To gain publicity or professional standing for performing the de-identification.**
301    Several successful re-identification efforts have been newsworthy and professionally
302    rewarding for the researchers conducting them.
303  - **To embarrass or harm the organization that performed the de-identification.**
304    Organizations that perform de-identification generally have an obligation to protect the
305    personal information contained in the original data. As such, demonstrating that their
306    privacy protecting measures were inadequate can embarrass or harm these organizations.
307  - **To gain direct benefit from the de-identified data.** For example, a marketing company
308    might purchase de-identified medical data and attempt to match up medical records with
309    identities, so that the re-individuals could be sent targeted coupons.

310  In the literature, re-identification attacks sometimes described as being performed by a
311  hypothetical *data intruder* who is in possession of the de-identified dataset and some additional
312  *background information.*

313  *Re-identification risk* is the measure of the risk that the identities and other information about
314  individuals in the data set will be learned from the de-identified data. It is hard to quantify this
315  risk, as the ability to re-identify depends on the original data set, the de-identification technique,
316  the technical skill of the data intruder, the intruder's available resources, and the availability of
317  additional data that can be linked with the de-identified data. In many cases the risk of re-
318  identification will increase over time as techniques improve and more background information
319  become available.

320  Researchers have taken various approaches for computing and reporting the re-identification risk
321  including:

322  - The risk that a specific person in the database can be re-identified. (The "prosecutor
323    scenario.")
324  - The risk that any person in the database can be re-identified. (The "journalist scenario.")
325  - The percentage of identities in the database that is actually re-identified.

326    • The distinguishability between an analysis performed on a database containing an
327      individual and on a database that does not contain the individual. (The "differential
328      identifiability" scenario.[16])

329    Likewise, different standards that have been used to describe the abilities of the "attacker"
330    including:

331    • A member of general public who has access to public information on the web
332    • A computer scientist skilled in re-identification ("expert")
333    • A member of the organization that produced the dataset ("insider")
334    • A friend or family member of the data subject
335    • The data subject ("self re-identification")

336    The purpose of de-identifying data is to allow some uses of the de-identified data while
337    providing for some privacy protection. These two goals are generally antagonistic, in that there is
338    a trade off between the amount of de-identification and the utility of the resulting data. The more
339    securely the data are de-identified, the less utility remains. In general, privacy protection
340    increases as more information is removed or modified from the original data set, but the
341    remaining data are less useful as a result. It is the responsibility of those de-identifying to
342    determine an acceptable trade-off.

343    A variety of harms that can result from the use or distribution of de-identified data, including:

344    • ***Incomplete de-identification.*** Identifiable private information may inadvertently remain
345      in the de-identified data set. This was the case in search query data released by AOL in
346      2006, in which journalists re-identified and contacted an AOL user through identifying
347      information that the user had typed as search queries.[17]
348    • ***Identity disclosure (***also called ***attribute disclosure*** and ***re-identification by linking).*** It
349      may be possible to re-identify specific records by linking some of the remaining data with
350      similar attributes in another, identifying data set.  De-identification is supposed to protect
351      against this harm.
352    • ***Inferential disclosure.*** If a data set reveals that all individuals who share a characteristic
353      have a particular attribute, and if the adversary knows of an individual in the sample who
354      has that characteristic, than that individual's attribute is exposed. For example, if a
355      hospital releases information showing that all 20-year-old female patients treated had a
356      specific diagnosis, and if Alice Smith is a 20-year-old female that is known to have been
357      treated at the hospital, then Alice Smith's diagnosis can be inferred, even though her

---

[16] Jaewoo Lee and Chris Clifton. 2012. Differential identifiability. In Proceedings of the 18th ACM SIGKDD international conference on Knowledge discovery and data mining (KDD '12). ACM, New York, NY, USA, 1041-1049. DOI=10.1145/2339530.2339695 http://doi.acm.org/10.1145/2339530.2339695

[17] Barbaro M, Zeller Jr. T. A Face Is Exposed for AOL Searcher No. 4417749 New York Times. 9 August, 2006.

358  individual de-identified medical records cannot be distinguished from the others.[18] In
359  general, de-identification is not designed to protect against inference-based attacks.

360  - *Association harms.* Even though it may not be possible to match a specific data record
361    with an individual, it may be possible to associate an individual with the dataset as a
362    whole or with a group of records within the dataset. That association may result in some
363    kind of stigma for the data subject.

364  - *Group harms.* Even if it is not possible to match up specific data records with
365    individuals, the data may be used to infer a characteristic and associate it with a group
366    represented in the data.

367  - *Unmasking.* If the data were pseudonymized, it may be possible reverse the
368    pseudonymization process. This might be done by using a table that shows the mapping
369    of the original identities to the pseudonyms, by reversing the pseudonymization
370    algorithm, or by performing a brute-force search in which the pseudonymization
371    algorithm is applied to every possible identity until the matching pseudonym is
372    discovered.

373  Organizations considering de-identification must therefore balance:

374  - The effort that the organization can spend performing and testing the de-identification
375    process.
376  - The utility desired for the de-identified data.
377  - The harms that might arise from the use of the de-identified data.
378  - The ability to use other controls that can minimize the risk.
379  - The likelihood that an attacker will attempt to re-identify the data, and the amount of
380    effort that the attacker might be willing to spend.

381  Privacy laws in the US tend to be concerned with regulating and thereby preventing the first two
382  categories of harms—the release of incompletely de-identified data, and assigning of an identity
383  to a specific record in the de-identified set. The other harms tend to be regulated by organizations
384  themselves, typically through the use of Institutional Review Boards or other kinds of internal
385  controls.

386  ## 2.5   Release models and data controls
387  One way to limit the chance of re-identification is to place controls on the way that the data may
388  be obtained and used. These controls can be classified according to different release models.
389  Several named models have been proposed in the literature, ranging from no restrictions to
390  tightly restricted. They are:

391  - **The Release and Forget model**[19]**:** The de-identified data may be released to the public,
392    typically by being published on the Internet. It can be difficult or impossible for an
393    organization to recall the data once released in this fashion.

---

[18] El Emam Methods for the de-identification of electronic health records for genomic research. Genome Medicine 2011, 3:25
http://genomemedicine.com/content/3/4/25

394          • **The Click-Through model**[20]: The de-identified data can are made available on the
395              Internet, but the user must agree in advance to some kind of "click-through" data use
396              agreement. In this event, an entity that performed and publicized a successful re-
397              identification attack might be subject to shaming or sanctions.
398          • **The Qualified Investigator model**[21]: The de-identified data may be made available to
399              qualified researchers under data use agreements. Typically these agreements prohibit
400              attempted re-identifying, redistribution, or contacting the data subjects.
401          • **The Enclave model**[22]: The de-identified data may be kept in some kind of segregated
402              enclave that accepts queries from qualified researchers, runs the queries on the de-
403              identified data, and responds with results. (This is an example of PPDM, rather than
404              PPDP.)

405   Gellman has proposed model legislation that would strengthen data use agreements.[23] Gellman's
406   proposal would recognize a new category of information *potentially identifiable personal*
407   *information (PI²)*. Consenting parties could add to their data-use agreement a promise from the
408   data provider that the data had been stripped of personal identifiers but still might be re-
409   identifiable. Recipients would then face civil and criminal penalties if they attempted to re-
410   identify. Thus, the proposed legislation would add to the confidence that de-identified data
411   would remain so. "Because it cannot be known at any time whether information is re-
412   identifiable, virtually all personal information that is not overtly identifiable is PI²," Gellman
413   notes.

## 3   Syntactic De-Identification Approaches and Their Criticism

415   *Syntactic de-identification techniques*[24] are techniques that attempt to de-identify by removing
416   specific data elements from a data set based on element type. This section introduces the
417   terminology used by such schemes, discusses the de-identification standard of the Health
418   Insurance Portability and Privacy Act (HIPAA) Privacy Rule, and discusses critiques of the
419   syntactic techniques and efforts that have appeared in the academic literature.

---

[19] Ohm, Paul, Broken Promises of Privacy: Responding to the Surprising Failure of Anonymization. UCLA Law Review, Vol.
      57, p. 1701, 2010

[20] K El Emam and B Malin, "Appendix B: Concepts and Methods for De-identifying Clinical Trial Data," in Sharing Clinical
      Trial Data: Maximizing Benefits, Minimizing Risk, Institute of Medicine of the National Academies, The National
      Academies Press, Washington, DC. 2015

[21] Ibid.

[22] Ibid.

[23] Gellman, Robert; "The Deidentification Dilemma: A Legislative and Contractual Proposal," July 12, 2010.

[24] Chris Clifton and Tamir Tassa, 2013. On Syntactic Anonymity and Differential Privacy. Trans. Data Privacy 6, 2 (August
      2013), 161-183.

420 **3.1   Removal of Direct Identifiers**
421 Syntactic de-identification approaches are easiest to understand when applied to a database
422 containing a single table of data. Each row contains data for a different individual.

423 ***Direct identifiers***, also called *directly identifying variables* and *direct identifying data*, are "data
424 that directly identifies a single individual." (ISO/TS 25237:2008) Examples of direct identifiers
425 include names, social security numbers and any "data that can be used to identify a person
426 without additional information or with cross-linking through other information that is in the
427 public domain."[25] Many practitioners treat information such as medical record numbers and
428 phone numbers as direct identifiers, even though additional information is required to link them
429 to an identity.

430 Direct identifiers must be removed or otherwise transformed during de-identification. This
431 processes is sometimes called *data masking*. There are at least three approaches for masking:

432     1) The direct identifiers can be removed.
433     2) The direct identifiers can be replaced with random values. If the same identify
434        appears twice, it receives two different values. This preserves the form of the original
435        data, allowing for some kinds of testing, but makes it harder to re-associate the data
436        with individuals.
437     3) The direct identifiers can be systematically replaced with pseudonyms, allowing
438        records referencing the same individual to be matched. Pseudonymization may also
439        allow for the identities to be unmasked at some time in the future if the mapping
440        between the direct identifiers and the pseudonyms is preserved or re-generated.

| Direct Identifiers | | | | | | | | |
|------|---------|----------|-----|-----|--------|-----------|-----|-----|
| Name | Address | Birthday | ZIP | Sex | Weight | Diagnosis | ... | ... |
|      |         |          |     |     |        |           |     |     |
|      |         |          |     |     |        |           |     |     |

441               **Table 1: A hypothetical data table showing direct identifiers**

442 Early efforts to de-identify databases stopped with the removal of direct identifiers.

443 **3.2   Re-identification through Linkage**
444 The *linkage attack* is the primary technique for re-identifying data that have been syntactically
445 de-identified. In this attack, each record in the de-identified dataset is linked with similar records
446 in a second dataset that contains both the linking information and the identity of the data subject.

447 Linkage attacks of this type were developed by Sweeney, who re-identified the medical records
448 of Massachusetts governor William Weld as part of her graduate work at MIT. At the time
449 Massachusetts was distributing a research database containing de-identified insurance

---

[25] ISO/TS 25237:2008(E), p.3

450   reimbursement records of Massachusetts state employees that had been hospitalized. To protect
451   the employees' privacy, their names were stripped from the database, but the employees' date of
452   birth, zip code, and sex was preserved to allow for statistical analysis.

453   Knowing that Weld had recently been treated at a Massachusetts hospital, Sweeney was able to
454   re-identify the governor's records by searching for the "de-identified" record that matched the
455   Governor's date of birth, zip code, and sex. She learned this information from the Cambridge
456   voter registration list, which she purchased for $20. Sweeney then generalized her findings,
457   arguing that up to 87% of the US population was uniquely identified by 5-digit ZIP code, date of
458   birth, and sex.[26]

459   Sweeney's linkage attack can be demonstrated graphically:

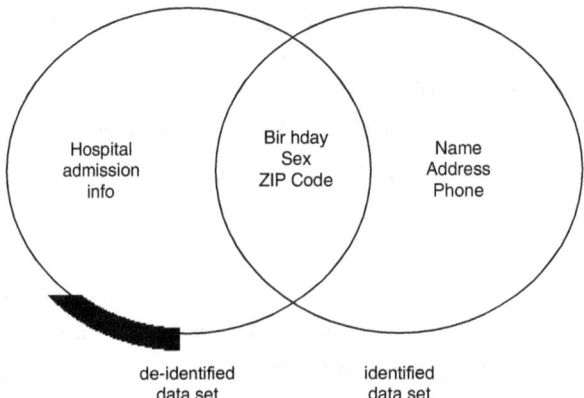

460

461              **Figure 2: Linkage attacks combine information from two or more data sets to re-identify records**

462   Many factors complicate such linkage attacks, however;

463       • In order to be linkable, a person needs to be in both data sets. Sweeney knew that Weld
464         was in both data sets.
465       • Only records that are uniquely distinguished by the linking variables in both sets can be
466         linked. In this case, a person's records can only be linked if no one else shares their same
467         birthday, sex and ZIP in either data set. As it turned out, no other person in Cambridge
468         shared Weld's date of birth.
469       • If the variables are not the same in both data sets, then the data must be normalized so
470         that they can be linked. This normalization can introduce errors. This was not an issue in
471         the Weld case, but it could be an issue if one dataset reported "age" and another reported
472         "birthday."
473       • Verifying whether or not a link is correct requires using information that was not used as
474         part of the linkage operation. In this case, Weld's medical records were verified using
475         newspaper accounts of what had happened.

---

[26] Sweeney L., Simple Demographics Often Identify People Uniquely, Carnegie Mellon University, Data Privacy Working Paper
    3, Pittsburgh, 2000. http://dataprivacylab.org/projects/identifiability/paper1.pdf

476 ## 3.3 De-identification of Quasi-Identifiers
477 ***Quasi-identifiers***, also called *indirect identifiers* or *indirectly identifying variables*, are
478 identifiers that by themselves do not identify a specific individual but can be aggregated and
479 "linked" with information in other data sets to identify data subjects. The re-identification of
480 William Weld's medical records demonstrated that birthday, ZIP, and Sex are quasi-identifiers.

| Direct Identifiers | | Quasi-Identifiers | | | | | | |
|---|---|---|---|---|---|---|---|---|
| Name | Address | Birthday | ZIP | Sex | Weight | Diagnosis | ... | ... |
| | | | | | | | | |
| | | | | | | | | |

481 **Table 2: A hypothetical data table showing direct identifiers and quasi-identifiers**

482 Quasi-identifiers pose a significant challenge for de-identification. Whereas direct identifiers can
483 be removed from the data set, quasi-identifiers generally convey some sort of information that
484 might be important for a later analysis. As such, they cannot be simply masked.

485 Several approaches have been proposed for de-identifying quasi-identifiers:

486    1) **Suppression:** The quasi-identifier can be suppressed or removed. Removing the data
487      maximizes privacy protection, but decreases the utility of the dataset.
488    2) **Generalization:** The quasi-identifier can be reported as being within a specific range
489      or as a member of a set. For example, the ZIP code 12345 could be generalized to a
490      ZIP code between 12000 and 12999. Generalization can be applied to the entire data
491      set or to specific records.
492    3) **Swapping:** Quasi-identifiers can be exchanged between records. Swapping must be
493      handled with care if it is necessary to preserve statistical properties.
494    4) **Sub-sampling.** Instead of releasing an entire data set, the de-identifying organization
495      can release a sample. If only subsample is released, the probability of re-identification
496      decreases.[27]

497 ***K-anonymity***[28] is a framework developed by Sweeney for quantifying the amount of
498 manipulation required of the quasi-identifiers to achieve a given desired level of privacy. The
499 technique is based on the concept of an ***equivalence class,*** the set of records that have the same
500 quasi-identifiers. A dataset is said to be *k-anonymous* if, for every combination of quasi-
501 identifiers, there are at least *k* matching records. For example, if a dataset that has the quasi-
502 identifiers birth year and state has k=4 anonymity, then there are at least four records for every
503 combination of (birth year, state) combination. Successive work has refined *k-anonymity* by

---

[27] El Emam, Methods for the de-identification of electronic health records for genomic research, Genome Medicine 2011, 3:25
http://genomemedicine.com/content/3/4/25

[28] Latanya Sweeney. 2002. *k*-anonymity: a model for protecting privacy. *Int. J. Uncertain. Fuzziness Knowl.-Based Syst.* 10, 5
(October 2002), 557-570. DOI=10.1142/S0218488502001648 http://dx.doi.org/10.1142/S0218488502001648

504    adding requirements for diversity of the sensitive attributes within each equivalence class[29], and
505    requiring that the resulting data are statistically close to the original data[30].

506    El Emam and Malin[31] have developed an 11-step process for de-identifying data based on the
507    identification of identifiers and quasi-identifiers:

508    - **Step 1: Determine direct identifiers in the data set.** An expert determines the elements
509      in the data set that serve only to identify the data subjects.
510    - **Step 2: Mask (transform) direct identifiers.** The direct identifiers are either removed or
511      replaced with pseudonyms.
512    - **Step 3: Perform threat modeling**. The organization determines "plausible adversaries,"
513      the additional information they might be able to use for re-identification, and the quasi-
514      identifiers that an adversary might use for re-identification.
515    - **Step 4: Determine minimal acceptable data utility.** In this step the organization
516      determines what uses can or will be made with the de-identified data, to determine the
517      maximal amount of de-identification that could take place.
518    - **Step 5: Determine the re-identification risk threshold.** The organization determines
519      acceptable risk for working with the data set and possibly mitigating controls.
520    - **Step 6: Import (sample) data from the source database.** Because the effort to acquire
521      data from the source (identified) database may be substantial, the authors recommend a
522      test data import run to assist in planning.
523    - **Step 7: Evaluate the actual re-identification risk.** The actual identification risk is
524      mathematically calculated.
525    - **Step 8: Compare the actual risk with the threshold.** The result of step 5 and step 7 are
526      compared.
527    - **Step 9: Set parameters and apply data transformations.** If the actual risk is less than
528      the minimal acceptable risk, the de-identification parameters are applied and the data is
529      transformed. If the risk is too high then new parameters or transformations need to be
530      considered.
531    - **Step 10: Perform diagnostics on the solution.** The de-identified data are tested to make
532      sure that it has sufficient utility and that re-identification is not possible within the
533      allowable parameters.
534    - **Step 11: Export transformed data to external data set.** Finally, the de-identified data
535      are exported and the de-identification techniques are documented in a written report.

---

[29] A. Machanavajjhala, J. Gehrke, D. Kifer, and M. Venkitasubramaniam. l-diversity: Privacy beyond k-anonymity. In Proc. 22nd Intnl. Conf. Data Engg. (ICDE), page 24, 2006.

[30] Ninghui Li, Tiancheng Li, and Suresh Venkatasubramanian (2007). "t-Closeness: Privacy beyond k-anonymity and l-diversity". ICDE (Purdue University).

[31] K. El Emam and B. Malin, "Appendix B: Concepts and Methods for De-identifying Clinical Trial Data," in Sharing Clinical Trial Data: Maximizing Benefits, Minimizing Risk, Institute of Medicine of the National Academies, The National Academies Press, Washington, DC. 2015

536 The chief criticism of de-identification based on direct identifiers and quasi-identifiers is that it is
537 difficult to determine which fields are identifying, and which are non-identifying data about the
538 data subjects. Aggarwal identified this problem in 2005, noting that when the data contains a
539 large number of attributes, "an exponential number of combinations of dimensions can be used
540 to make precise inference attacks... [W]hen a data set contains a large number of attributes
541 which are open to inference attacks, we are faced with a choice of either completely suppressing
542 most of the data or losing the desired level of anonymity."[32]

543 Work since has demonstrated some of Aggarwal's concerns: many seemingly innocuous data
544 fields can become identifying for an adversary that has the appropriate matching information
545 (see Section 3.5). Furthermore, values that cannot be used as quasi-identifiers today may become
546 quasi-identifiers in the future as additional datasets are developed and released. To accurately
547 assess re-identification risk, it is therefore necessary to accurately model the knowledge,
548 determination, and computational resources of the adversaries that will be attempting the re-
549 identification.

550 ### 3.4    De-identification of Protected Health Information (PHI) under HIPAA
551 The Health Insurance Portability and Accountability Act of 1996 (HIPAA) Privacy Rule
552 describes two approaches for de-identifying Protected Health Information (PHI): The Expert
553 Determination Method (§164.514(b)(1)) and the Safe Harbor method (§164.514(b)(2)).

554 The "Expert Determination" method provides for an expert to examine the data and determine an
555 appropriate means for de-identification that would minimize the risk of re-identification. The
556 specific language of the Privacy Rule states:

557       "(1) A person with appropriate knowledge of and experience with generally accepted
558       statistical and scientific principles and methods for rendering information not individually
559       identifiable:
560        (i) Applying such principles and methods, determines that the risk is very small that the
561       information could be used, alone or in combination with other reasonably available
562       information, by an anticipated recipient to identify an individual who is a subject of the
563       information; and
564        (ii) Documents the methods and results of the analysis that justify such determination;
565       or"

566 The "Safe Harbor" method allows a covered entity to treat data as de-identified if it by removing
567 18 specific types of data for "the individual or relatives, employers, or household members of the
568 individual." The 18 types are:

569       "(A) Names
570       (B) All geographic subdivisions smaller than a state, including street address, city,
571       county, precinct, ZIP code, and their equivalent geocodes, except for the initial three
572       digits of the ZIP code if, according to the current publicly available data from the Bureau

---

[32] Charu C. Aggarwal. 2005. On *k*-anonymity and the curse of dimensionality. In *Proceedings of the 31st international conference on Very large data bases* (VLDB '05). VLDB Endowment 901-909.

573     of the Census:
574         (1) The geographic unit formed by combining all ZIP codes with the same three initial
575     digits contains more than 20,000 people; and
576         (2) The initial three digits of a ZIP code for all such geographic units containing 20,000
577     or fewer people is changed to 000
578     (C) All elements of dates (except year) for dates that are directly related to an individual,
579     including birth date, admission date, discharge date, death date, and all ages over 89 and
580     all elements of dates (including year) indicative of such age, except that such ages and
581     elements may be aggregated into a single category of age 90 or older
582     (D) Telephone numbers
583     (E) Fax numbers
584     (F) Email addresses
585     (G) Social security numbers
586     (H) Medical record numbers
587     (I) Health plan beneficiary numbers
588     (J) Account numbers
589     (K) Certificate/license numbers
590     (L) Vehicle identifiers and serial numbers, including license plate numbers
591     (M) Device identifiers and serial numbers
592     (N) Web Universal Resource Locators (URLs)
593     (O) Internet Protocol (IP) addresses
594     (P) Biometric identifiers, including finger and voiceprints
595     (Q) Full-face photographs and any comparable images
596     (R) Any other unique identifying number, characteristic, or code, except as permitted by
597     paragraph (c) of this section [Paragraph (c) is presented below in the section "Re-
598     identification"];"
599

600     In addition to removing these data, the covered entity must not "have actual knowledge that the
601     information could be used alone or in combination with other information to identify an
602     individual who is a subject of the information."

603     The Privacy Rule is heavily influenced by Sweeny's research, as evidenced by its citation of
604     Sweeny's research the rule's specific attention to the quasi-identifiers identified by Sweeny (ZIP
605     code and birthdate) for generalization. The Privacy Rule strikes a balance between the risk of re-
606     identification and the need to retain some utility in the data set—for example, by allowing the
607     reporting of the first 3 digits of the ZIP code and the year of birth. Researchers have estimated
608     that properly applied, the HIPAA Safe Harbor rule seems to allow the identification probability
609     of approximately 1.5%.[33]

610     The actual rate of re-identification may be lower in some cases. In 2010 the Office of the
611     National Coordinator for Health Information Technology (ONC HIT) at the US Department of
612     Health and Human Services conducted a test of the HIPAA de-identification standard. As part of

---

[33] Jaewoo Lee and Chris Clifton, Differential Identifiability, KDD '12, Aug. 12-16, 2012. Bejing, China.

613    the study, researchers were provided with 15,000 hospital admission records belonging to
614    Hispanic individuals from a hospital system between 2004 and 2009. Researchers then attempted
615    to match the de-identified records to a commercially available data set of 30,000 records from
616    InfoUSA. Based on the Census data the researchers estimated that the 30,000 commercial
617    records covered approximately 5,000 of the hospital patients. When the experimenters matched
618    using Sex, ZIP3 (the first 3 digits of the ZIP code, as allowed by HIPAA), and Age, they found
619    216 unique records in the hospital data, 84 unique records in the InfoUSA data, and only 20
620    records that matched on both sides. They then attempted to confirm these matches with the
621    hospital and found that only 2 were actual matches, which were defined as having the same 5-
622    digit ZIP code, the same last name, same street address, and same phone number. This represents
623    a re-identification rate of 0.013%; the researchers also calculate a more conservative re-
624    identification risk of 0.22%.

625    HIPAA also allows the sharing of *limited data sets* that have been partially de-identified but still
626    include dates, city, state, zip code, and age. Such data sets may only be shared for research,
627    public health, or health care operations, and may only be shared with if a data use agreement is
628    executed between the covered entities to assure for subject privacy.[34] At minimum, the data use
629    agreements must require security safeguards, require that all users of the data be similarly
630    limited, and prohibit contacting of the data subjects.

### 3.5    Evaluation of Syntactic De-identification
632    The basic assumption of syntactic de-identification is that some of the columns in a data set
633    might contain useful information without being inherently identifying. In recent years a
634    significant body of academic research has shown that this assumption is not true in some cases.

635    •   *Netflix Prize:* Narayanan and Shmatikov showed in 2008 that in many cases the set of
636        movies that a person had watched could be used as an identifier.[35] Netflix had released a
637        de-identified data set of movies that some of its customers had watched and ranked as
638        part of its "Netflix Prize" competition. The researchers showed that a set common movies
639        could be used to link many records in the Netflix dataset with similar records in the
640        Internet Movie Data Base (IMDB), which had not been de-identified.  The threat scenario
641        is that by rating a few movies on IMDB, a person might inadvertently reveal *all* of the
642        movies that they had watched, since the IMDB data could be linked with the public data
643        from the Netflix Prize.

645    •   *Medical Tests:* Atreya et al. showed in 2013 that 5-7 laboratory results from a patient
646        could be used "as a search key to discover the corresponding record in a de-identified
647        biomedical research database."[36] Using a dataset with 8.5 million laboratory results from

---

[34] http://privacyruleandresearch nih.gov/pr_08.asp

[35] Narayanan, Arvind and Shmatikov Vitaly: Robust De-anonymization of Large Sparse Datasets. IEEE Symposium on Security
     and Privacy 2008: 111-125

[36] Atreya, Ravi V, Joshua C Smith,Allison B McCoy, Bradley Malin and Randolph A Miller, "Reducing patient re-identification
     risk for laboratory results within research datasets," J Am Med Inform Assoc 2013;20:95–101. doi:10.1136/amiajnl-2012-
     001026.

648     61,280 patients, the researchers found that four consecutive laboratory test results
649     uniquely identified between 34% and 100% of the population, depending on the test. The
650     two most common test results, CHEM7 and CBC, respectively identified 98.9% and
651     98.8% of the test subjects. The threat scenario is that a person who intercepted a single
652     lab identified lab report containing a CHEM7 or CBC result could use report to search
653     the de-identified biomedical research database for other records belonging to the
654     individual.
655

656     • **Mobility Traces:** Also in 2013, Montjoye et al. showed that people and vehicles could be
657       identified by their "mobility traces" (a record of locations and times that the person or
658       vehicle visited). In their study, trace data for 1.5 million individuals was processed, with
659       time values being generalized to the hour and spatial data generalized to the resolution
660       provided by a cell phone system (typically 10-20 city blocks). The researchers found that
661       four randomly chosen observations of an individual putting them at a specific place and
662       time was sufficient to uniquely identify 95% of the data subjects.[37] Space/time points for
663       individuals can be collected from a variety of sources, including purchases with a credit
664       card, a photograph, or Internet usage. A similar study performed by Ma et al. found that
665       30%-50% of individuals could be identified with 10 pieces of side information.[38] The
666       threat scenario is that person who revealed 5 place/time pairs (perhaps by sending email
667       from work and home at four times over the course of a month) would make it possible for
668       an attacker to identify their entire mobility trace in a publicly released data set.
669

670     • **Taxi Ride Data:** In 2014 The New York City Taxi and Limousine Commission released a
671       dataset containing a record of every New York City taxi trip in 2013 (173 million in
672       total). The data did not include the names of the taxi drivers or riders, but it did include a
673       32-digit alphanumeric code that could be readily converted to each taxi's medallion
674       number. A data scientist intern at the company Neustar discovered that he could find
675       time-stamped photographs on the web of celebrities entering or leaving taxis in which the
676       medallion was clearly visible.[39] With this information the was able to discover the other
677       end-point of the ride, the amount paid, and the amount tipped for two of the 173 million
678       taxi rides. A reporter at the Gawker website was able to identify another nine. [40]

679     The experience with the Netflix Prize indicates and the laboratory results shows that many sets

---

[37] Yves-Alexandre de Montjoye et al., Unique in the Crowd: The privacy bounds of human mobility, Scientific Reports 3 (2013), Article 1376.

[38] Ma, C.Y.T.; Yau, D.K.Y.; Yip, N.K.; Rao, N.S.V., "Privacy Vulnerability of Published Anonymous Mobility Traces," Networking, IEEE/ACM Transactions on , vol.21, no.3, pp.720,733, June 2013

[39] "Riding with the Stars: Passenger Privacy in the NYC Taxicab Dataset," Anthony Tockar, September 15, 2014, http://research.neustar.biz/author/atockar/

[40] "Public NYC Taxicab Database Lets you See How Celebrities Tip," J. K. Trotter, GAWKER, October 23, 2014. http://gawker.com/the-public-nyc-taxicab-database-that-accidentally-track-1646724546

680    of sensitive values might also be identifying, provided that there is sufficient range or diversity
681    for the identifiers in the population. The experience with the taxi data shows that there are many
682    unanticipated sources of data that might correlate with other information in the data record.

683    The taxi and mobility trace studies demonstrate the strong identification power of geospatial
684    information. Since each person can only be at one place at one time, just a few observations of a
685    person's location and time can be highly identifying, even in a data set that generalized and
686    noisy. Furthermore, some locations are highly identifying—either because they are isolated or
687    well photographed.

688    However, the medical tests and taxi studies also show that relatively small changes to the data
689    may make re-identification difficult or impossible. Atreya et al. demonstrated this directly. In
690    the case of the Taxi data, the celebrities were only identified because the taxi medallion number
691    pseudonymization could be unmasked, and the main privacy impact was the release of the
692    specific geographical locations and tip amounts. If the medallion number had been properly
693    protected and if the GPS location data had be aggregated to a 100 meter square grid, the risk of
694    re-identification would have been considerably reduced. As it was, the taxi data demonstrates
695    that the risk of re-identification under the "journalist scenario" (which sees any failure as a
696    significant shortcoming) may be high, but risk under the "prosecutor scenario" might be very
697    low (11 out of 173 million).

698    Putting this information into context of real-world de-identification requirements is difficult. For
699    example, the ONC HIT 2010 study only attempted to match using the specific quasi-identifiers
700    anticipated by the HIPAA Privacy Rule—age in years, sex, and ZIP3. Atreya et al. used a
701    different threat model, one in which the attacker was assumed to have the results of a laboratory
702    test. The results of Atreya imply that *if* the ONC HIT study included laboratory test results, and *if*
703    the attacker had a laboratory test report including the patient's name and seven or more test
704    results, then there is an overwhelming probability that there is a specific set of records in the de-
705    identified data that are an exact match. However, this test was never done, and many may feel
706    that it is not a realistic threat model.

707    El Emam et al[41] reviewed 14 re-identification attempts published between 2001 and 2010. For
708    each the authors determined whether or not health data had been included, the profession of the
709    adversary, the country where the re-identification took place, the percentage of the records that
710    had been re-identified, the standards that were followed for de-identification, and whether or not
711    the re-identification had been verified. The researchers found that the successful re-identification
712    events typically involved small data sets that had not been de-identified according to existing
713    standards. As such, drawing scientific conclusions from these cases is difficult. In many cases
714    the re-identification attackers have re-identified just a few records but stated that many more
715    could be re-identified.

716    De-identification and PPDP are still possible, but require a more nuanced attention to the
717    potential for re-identification of the data subjects. One approach is to treat all data in the dataset

---

[41] K El Emam, E Jonker, L Arbuckle, B MalinB (2011) A Systematic Review of Re-Identification Attacks on Health Data. PLoS
    ONE 6(12): e28071. doi:10.1371/journal.pone.0028071

718    as quasi-identifiers and accordingly manipulate them to protect privacy. This is possible, but may
719    require developing specific technology for each different data type. For example, Atreya et al.
720    developed an "expert" algorithm that could de-identify the data by perturbing the test results with
721    minimal impact on diagnostic accuracy.[42]

### 3.6   Alternatives to Syntactic De-identification

723    An alternative to syntactic de-identification is to generate synthetic data or synthetic data sets
724    that are statistically similar to the original data but which cannot be de-identified because they
725    are not based on actual people. Synthetic data elements are widely used in statistical disclosure
726    controls—for example, by aggregating data into categories, suppressing individual cells, adding
727    noise, or swapping data between similar records.

## 4   Challenges in De-Identifying Contextual Data

729    Whereas the last chapter was concerned mostly with the de-identification of tabular or structured
730    data, this section concerns itself with the open challenges of de-identifying contextual data.

### 4.1   De-identifying medical text

732    Medical records contain significant amounts of unstructured text. In recent years there has been a
733    significant effort to develop and evaluate tools designed to remove the 18 HIPAA data elements
734    from free-format text using natural language processing techniques. The two primary techniques
735    explored have been rule-based systems and statistical systems. Rule-based systems tend to work
736    well for specific kinds of text but do not work well when applied to new domains. Statistical
737    tools generally perform less accurately and require labeled training data, but are easier to
738    repurpose to new domains.

739    Multiple factors combine to make de-identifying text narratives hard:

740       1)  Direct identifiers such as names and addresses may not be clearly marked.
741       2)  Important medical information may be mistaken for personal information and
742           removed. This is especially a problem for eponyms which are commonly used in
743           medicine to describe diseases (e.g. Addison's Disease, Bell's Palsy, Reiter's
744           Syndrome, etc.)
745       3)  Even after the removal of the 18 HIPAA elements, information may remain that
746           allows identification of the medical subject.
747       4)  Medical information currently being released as "de-identified" frequently does not
748           conform to the HIPAA standard.

749    In general the best systems seem to exhibit overall accuracy between 95-98% compared to
750    human annotators. A study by Meystre, Shen et. al showed the automatically de-identified
751    records from the Veteran's Administration were not recognized by the patient's treating
752    professional.[43]

---

[42] Atreya, *supra*.

[43] Meystre S et al., Can Physicians Recognize Their Own Patients in De-Identified Notes? In Health – For Continuity of Care C.

753    Several researchers have performed formal evaluations of de-identification tools:

754    • In 2012 Deleger et al at Cincinnati Children's Hospital Medical Center tested The
755       MITRE Identification Scrubber Toolkit (MIST)[44] against MCRF, an in-house system
756       developed by CCHMC based on the MALLET machine-learning package. The reference
757       corpora were 3503 clinical notes selected from 5 million notes created at CCHMC in
758       2010, the 2006 i2b2 de-identification challenge corpus,[45] and the PhisyoNet corpus.[46][47]
759

760    • In 2013 Ferrández *et al* at the University of Utah Department of Biomedical Informatics
761       performed an evaluation of five automated de-identification systems against two
762       reference corpora. The test was conducted with the 2006 i2b2 de-identification challenge
763       corpus, consisting of 889 documents that had been de-identification and then given
764       synthetic data,[48] and a corpus of 800 documents provided by the Veterans Administration
765       that was randomly drawn from documents with more than 500 words dated between
766       4/01/2008 and 3/31/2009.
767

768    • In 2013 The National Library of Medicine issued a report to its Board of Scientific
769       Counselors entitled "Clinical Text De-Identification Research" in which the NLM
770       compared the performance of its internally developed tool, the NLM Scrubber (NLM-S),
771       with the MIT de-identification system (MITdeid) and MIST.[49] The test was conduct with
772       an internal corpus of 1073 Physician Observation Reports and 2020 Patient Study
773       Reports from the NIH Clinical Center.
774


775    Both the CCHMC and the University of Utah studies tested the systems "out-of-the-box" and
776    after they were tuned by using part of the corpus as training data. The Utah study found that
777    none of the de-identification tools worked well enough to de-identify the VHA records for public
778    release, and that the rule-based systems exceled for finding certain kinds of information (e.g.
779    SSNs and phone numbers), while the trainable systems worked better for other kinds of data.

---

Lovis et al. (Eds.) © 2014 European Federation for Medical Informatics and IOS Press.

[44] Aberdeen J, Bayer S, Yeniterzi R, et al. The MITRE Identification Scrubber Toolkit: design, training, and assessment. Int J Med Inform 2010;79:849e59.

[45] Uzuner O, Luo Y, Szolovits P. Evaluating the state-of-the-art in automatic de- identification. J Am Med Inform Assoc 2007;14:550e63.

[46] Neamatullah I, Douglass MM, Lehman LW, et al. Automated de-identification of free-text medical records. BMC Med Inform Decis Mak 2008;8:32.

[47] Goldberger AL, Amaral LA, Glass L, et al. PhysioBank, PhysioToolkit, and Physionet: components of a new research resource for complex physiologic signals. Circulation 2000;101:E215e20.

[48] Uzuner O, Luo Y, Szolovits P. Evaluating the state-of-the-art in automatic de- identification. J Am Med Inform Assoc 2007;14:550e63.

[49] Kayaalp M et al, A report to the Board of Scientific Counselors, 2013, The Lister Hill National Center for Biomedical Communications, National Library of Medicine.

780    Although there are minor variations between the systems, they are all had similar performance.
781    The NLM study found that NLM-S significantly outperformed MIST and MITdeid on the NLM
782    data set, removing 99.2% of the tokens matching the HIPAA Privacy Rule. The authors
783    concluded that the remaining tokens would not pose a significant threat to patient privacy.

784    It should be noted that none of these systems attempt to de-identify data beyond removal of the
785    18 HIPAA data elements, leaving the possibility that individuals could be re-identified using
786    other information. For example, regulations in both the US and Canada require reporting of
787    adverse drug interactions. These reports have been re-identified by journalists and researchers by
788    correlating reports of fatalities with other data sources, such as news reports and death registers.

789    **4.2   De-identifying Imagery**
790    Multimedia imagery such as still photographs, consumer videos and surveillance video pose
791    special de-identification challenges because of the wealth of identity information they potentially
792    contain. Similar issues come into play when de-identifying digital still imagery, video, and
793    medical imagery (X-Rays, MRI scans, etc.)

794    In general there are a three specific identification concerns:

795        1)  The image itself may contain the individual's name on a label that is visible to a
796             human observer but readily difficult to detect programmatically.
797        2)  The file format may contain metadata that specifically identifies the individual. For
798             example, there may be a GPS address of the person's house, or the person's name
799             may be embedded in a header.
800        3)  The image may contain an identifying biometric such as a scar, a hand measurement,
801             or a specific injury.

802    Early research had the goal of producing images in which the faces could not be reliably
803    identified by face recognition systems. In many cases this is sufficient: blurring is used by
804    Google Street View, one of the largest deployments of photo de-identification technology.[50]
805    Google claims that its completely automatic system is able to blur 89% of faces and 94-96% of
806    license plates. Nevertheless, journalists have criticized Google for leaving many faces
807    unblurred[51] and for blurring the faces of religious effigies[52],[53].

808    Some researchers have developed systems that can identify and blur bodies,[54] as research has

---

[50] Frome, Andrea, et al, "Large-scale Privacy Protection in Google Street View," IEEE International Conference on Computer Vision (2009).

[51] Stephen Chapman, "Google Maps, Street View, and privacy: Try harder, Google," ZDNet, January 31, 2013. http://www.zdnet.com/article/google-maps-street-view-and-privacy-try-harder-google/

[52] Gonzalez, Robbie. "The Faceless Gods of Google Street View," io9, October 4, 2014. http://io9.com/the-faceless-gods-of-google-street-view-1642462649

[53] Brownlee, John, "The Anonymous Gods of Google Street View," Fast Company, October 7, 2014. http://www.fastcodesign.com/3036319/the-anonymous-gods-of-google-street-view#3

[54] Prachi Agrawal and P. J. Narayanan. 2009. Person de-identification in videos. In Proceedings of the 9th Asian conference on

809  shown that bodies are frequently identifiable without faces.[55] An experimental system can locate
810  and remove identifying tattoos from still images.[56]

811  Blurring and pixilation have the disadvantage of creating a picture that is visually jarring. Care
812  must be taken if pixilation or blurring are used for obscuring video, however, as technology
813  exists for de-pixelating and de-blurring video by combining multiple images. To address this,
814  some researchers have developed systems that can replace faces with a composite face,[57,58] or
815  with a face that is entirely synthetic.[59,60]

816  Quantifying the effectiveness of these algorithms is difficult. While some researchers may score
817  the algorithms against face recognition software, other factors such as clothing, body pose, or
818  geo-temporal setting might make the person identifiable by associates or themselves. A proper
819  test of image de-identification should therefore include a variety of re-identification scenarios.

820  ### 4.3    De-identifying Genetic sequences and biological materials
821  Genetic sequences are not considered to be personally identifying information by HIPAA's de-
822  identification rule. Nevertheless, because genetic information is inherited, genetic sequences
823  have been identified through the use of genetic databanks even if the individual was not
824  previously sequenced and placed in an identification database.

825  In 2005 a 15-year-old teenager used the DNA-testing service FamilyTreeDNA.com to find his
826  sperm donor father. The service, which cost $289, did not identify the boy's father, but it did
827  identify two men who had matching Y-chromosomes. The two men had the same surname but
828  with different spellings. As the Y-Chromosome is passed directly from father to son with no
829  modification, it tends to be inherited the same way as European surnames. With this information
830  and with the sperm donor's date and place of birth (which had been provided to the boy's

---

Computer Vision - Volume Part III (ACCV'09), Hongbin Zha, Rin-ichiro Taniguchi, and Stephen Maybank (Eds.), Vol. Part III. Springer-Verlag, Berlin, Heidelberg, 266-276. DOI=10.1007/978-3-642-12297-2_26 http://dx.doi.org/10.1007/978-3-642-12297-2_26

[55] Rice, Phillips, et al., Unaware Person Recognition From the Body when Face Identification Fails, Psychological Science, November 2013, vol. 24, no. 11, 2235-2243 http://pss.sagepub.com/content/24/11/2235

[56] Darijan Marčetić et al., An Experimental Tattoo De-identification System for Privacy Protection in Still Images, MIPRO 2014, 26-30 May 2014, Opatija, Croatia

[57] Ralph Gross, Latanya Sweeney, Jeffrey Cohn, Fernando de la Torre, and Simon Baker. In: Protecting Privacy in Video Surveillance, A. Senior, editor. Springer, 2009 Preserving Privacy by De-identifying Facial Images. http://dataprivacylab.org/projects/facedeid/paper.pdf

[58] E. Newton, L. Sweeney, and B. Malin. Preserving Privacy by De-identifying Facial Images, Carnegie Mellon University, School of Computer Science, Technical Report, CMU-CS-03-119. Pittsburgh: March 2003.

[59] Saleh Mosaddegh, Löic Simon, Frederic Jurie. Photorealistic Face de-Identification by Aggregating Donors' Face Components. Asian Conference on Computer Vision, Nov 2014, Singapore. pp.1-16.

[60] Umar Mohammed, Simon J. D. Prince, and Jan Kautz. 2009. Visio-lization: generating novel facial images. In ACM SIGGRAPH 2009 papers (SIGGRAPH '09), Hugues Hoppe (Ed.). ACM, New York, NY, USA, Article 57, 8 pages. DOI=10.1145/1576246.1531363 http://doi.acm.org/10.1145/1576246.1531363

831    mother), the boy was able to identify his father using an online search service.[61]

832    In 2013 a group of researchers at MIT extended the experiment, identifying surnames and
833    complete identities of more than 50 individuals who had DNA tests released on the Internet as
834    part of the Study of Human Polymorphisms (CEPH) project and the 1000 Genomes Project.[62]

835    At the present time there is no scientific consensus on the minimum size of a genetic sequence
836    necessary for re-identification. There is also no consensus on an appropriate mechanism to make
837    de-identified genetic information available to researchers without the need to execute a data use
838    agreement.

839    ## 4.4    De-identification of geographic and map data
840    De-identification of geographic data is not well researched. Current methods rely on perturbation
841    and generalization. Perturbation is problematical in some cases, because perturbed locations can
842    become nonsensical (e.g. moving a restaurant into a body of water). Generalization may not be
843    sufficient to hide identity, however, especially if the population is sparse or if multiple
844    observations can be correlated.

845    However, without some kind of generalization or perturbation there is so much diversity in
846    geographic data that it may be impossible to de-identify locations. For example, measurement of
847    cell phone accelerometers taken over a time period can be used to infer position by fitting
848    movements to a street grid.[63] This is of concern because the Android and iOS operating systems
849    do not consider accelerometers to be sensitive information.

850    ## 4.5    Estimation of Re-identification Risk
851    Practitioners are in need of easy-to-use procedures for calculating the risk of re-identification
852    given a specific de-identification protocol. Calculating this risk is complicated, as it depends on
853    many factors, including the distinctiveness of different individuals within the sampled data set,
854    the de-identification algorithm, the availability of linkage data, and the range of individuals that
855    might mount a re-identification attack.

856    There are also different kinds of re-identification risk. A model might report the average risk of
857    each subject being identified, the risk that *any* subject will be identified, the risk that individual
858    subjects might be identified as being 1 of $k$ different individuals, etc.

859    Danker et al. propose a statistical model and decision rule for estimating the distinctiveness of
860    different kinds of data sources.[64] El Emam et al. developed a technique for modeling the risk of

---

[61] Sample, Ian. Teenager finds sperm donor dad on internet. The Guardian, November 2, 2005.
        http://www.theguardian.com/science/2005/nov/03/genetics.news

[62] Gymrek et al, Identifying Personal Genomes by Surname Inference, Science 18 Jan 2013, 339:6117.

[63] Jun Han; Owusu, E.; Nguyen, L.T.; Perrig, A.; Zhang, J., "ACComplice: Location inference using accelerometers on
        smartphones," *Communication Systems and Networks (COMSNETS), 2012 Fourth International Conference on*, pp.1,9, 3-7
        Jan. 2012

[64] Dankar et al. Estimating the re-identification risk of clinical data sets, BMC Medical Informatics and Decision Making 2012,
        12:66.

861 re-identifying adverse drug event reports based on two attacker models: a "mildly motivated
862 adversary" whose goal is to identify a single record, and a "highly motivated adversary" that
863 wishes to identify and verify all matches, "and is only limited by practical or financial
864 considerations."[65]

865 Practitioners are also in need of standards for acceptable risk. As previously noted, researchers
866 have estimated that properly applied, the HIPAA Safe Harbor rule seems to allow the
867 identification probability of approximately 1.5%.[66] El Emam and Alvarez are critical of the
868 "Article 29 Working Party Opinion 05/2014 on data anonymization techniques" because the
869 document appears to only endorse de-identification techniques that produce zero risk of re-
870 identification.[67]

## 5 Conclusion

872 De-identification techniques can reduce or limit the privacy harms resulting from the release of a
873 data set, while still providing users of the data with some utility.

874 To date, the two primary harms associated with re-identification appear to be damage to the
875 reputation of the organization that performed the de-identification, and the discovery of private
876 facts of people who were re-identified. Researchers or journalists performed most of the
877 publicized re-identifications, and many of those re-identified were public figures.

878 Organizations sharing de-identified information should assure that they do not leave quasi-
879 identifiers in the dataset that could readily be used for re-identification. They should also survey
880 for the existence of linkable databases. Finally, organizations may wish to consider controls on
881 the de-identified agreements that prohibit re-identification, including click-through licenses and
882 appropriate data use agreements.

## Appendix A   Glossary

884 Selected terms used in the publication are defined below. Where noted, the definition is sourced
885 to another publication.

886 **aggregated information:** Information elements collated on a number of individuals, typically
887 used for the purposes of making comparisons or identifying patterns. (SP800-122)

888 **confidentiality:** "Preserving authorized restrictions on information access and disclosure,

---

[65] El Emam et al., Evaluating the risk of patient re-identification from adverse drug event reports, BMC Medical Informatics and Decision Making 2013, 13:114 http://www.biomedcentral.com/1472-6947/13/114

[66] Jaewoo Lee and Chris Clifton, Differential Identifiability, KDD '12, Aug. 12-16, 2012. Bejing, China.

[67] Khaled El Emam and Cecelia Álvarez, A critical appraisal of the Article 29 Working Party Opinion 05/2014 on data anonymization techniques, International Data Privacy Law, 2015, Vol. 5, No. 1

889 including means for protecting personal privacy and proprietary information."[68]‖(SP800-122)

890 **Context of Use:** The purpose for which PII is collected, stored, used, processed, disclosed, or
891 disseminated. (SP800-122)

892 **data linking:** "matching and combining data from multiple databases." (ISO/TS 25237:2008)

893 **De-identification:** "General term for any process of removing the association between a set of
894 identifying data and the data subject." (ISO/TS 25237-2008)

895 **De-identified Information:** Records that have had enough PII removed or obscured such that
896 the remaining information does not identify an individual and there is no reasonable basis to
897 believe that the information can be used to identify an individual. (SP800-122)

898 **direct identifying data:** "data that directly identifies a single individual." (ISO/TS 25237:2008)

899 **Distinguishable Information:** Information that can be used to identify an individual. (SP800-
900 122)

901 **Harm:** Any adverse effects that would be experienced by an individual (i.e., that may be
902 socially, physically, or financially damaging) or an organization if the confidentiality of PII were
903 breached. (SP800-122)

904 **Healthcare identifier:** "identifier of a person for exclusive use by a healthcare system." (ISO/TS
905 25237:2008)

906 **HIPAA Privacy Rule:** "establishes national standards to protect individuals' medical records
907 and other personal health information and applies to health plans, health care clearinghouses, and
908 those health care providers that conduct certain health care transactions electronically." (HHS
909 OCR 2014)

910 **identifiable person:** "one who can be identified, directly or indirectly, in particular by reference
911 to an identification number or to one or more factors specific to his physical, physiological,
912 mental, economic, cultural or social identity." (ISO/TS 25237:2008)

913 **identifier** "information used to claim an identity, before a potential corroboration by a
914 corresponding authenticator." (ISO/TS 25237:2008)

915 **Limited data set:** A partially de-identified data set containing health information and some
916 identifying information including complete dates, age to the nearest hour, city, state, and
917 complete ZIP code.

918 **Linkable Information:** Information about or related to an individual for which there is a
919 possibility of logical association with other information about the individual. (SP800-122)

---

[68] 44 U.S.C. § 3542, http://uscode house.gov/download/pls/44C35.txt.

920 **Linked Information:** Information about or related to an individual that is logically associated
921 with other information about the individual. (SP800-122)

922 **Obscured Data:** Data that has been distorted by cryptographic or other means to hide
923 information. It is also referred to as being masked or obfuscated. (SP800-122)

924 **personal identifier:** "information with the purpose of uniquely identifying a person within a
925 given context." (ISO/TS 25237:2008)

926 **personal data:** "any information relating to an identified or identifiable natural person ("data
927 subject")" (ISO/TS 25237:2008)

928 **Personally Identifiable Information (PII):** —"Any information about an individual maintained
929 by an agency, including (1) any information that can be used to distinguish or trace an
930 individual's identity, such as name, social security number, date and place of birth, mother's
931 maiden name, or biometric records; and (2) any other information that is linked or linkable to an
932 individual, such as medical, educational, financial, and employment information."[69] (SP800-122)

933 **PII Confidentiality Impact Level:** The PII confidentiality impact level—low, moderate, or
934 high—indicates the potential harm that could result to the subject individuals and/or the
935 organization if PII were inappropriately accessed, used, or disclosed. (SP800-122)

936 **Privacy:** "freedom from intrusion into the private life or affairs of an individual when that
937 intrusion results from undue or illegal gathering and use of data about that individual." [ISO/IEC
938 2382-8:1998, definition 08-01-23]

939 **Privacy Impact Assessment (PIA):** "An analysis of how information is handled that ensures
940 handling conforms to applicable legal, regulatory, and policy requirements regarding privacy;
941 determines the risks and effects of collecting, maintaining and disseminating information in
942 identifiable form in an electronic information system; and examines and evaluates protections
943 and alternative processes for handling information to mitigate potential privacy risks."[70] (SP800-
944 122)‖

945 **Protected Health Information:**

946 **Pseudonymization:** "particular type of anonymization that both removes the association with a
947 data subject and adds an association between a particular set of characteristics relating to the data
948 subject and one or more pseudonyms." [ISO/TS 25237:2008]

949 **Pseudonym:** "personal identifier that is different from the normally used personal identifier."
950 [ISO/TS 25237:2008]

---

[69] GAO Report 08-536, Privacy: Alternatives Exist for Enhancing Protection of Personally Identifiable Information, May 2008,
http://www.gao.gov/new.items/d08536.pdf

[70] OMB M-03-22.

951    **Recipient:** "natural or legal person, public authority, agency or any other body to whom data are
952    disclosed." [ISO/TS 25237:2008]

953    ## Appendix B    Resources

954    ### B.1    Official publications

955    AU:

956    • Office of the Australian Information Commissioner, *Privacy business resource 4: De-*
957    *identification of data and information*, Australian Government, April 2014.
958    http://www.oaic.gov.au/images/documents/privacy/privacy-resources/privacy-business-
959    resources/privacy_business_resource_4.pdf

960    EU:

961    • Article 29 Data Protection Working Party, 0829/14/EN WP216, Opinion 05/2014 on
962    Anonymisation Techniques, Adopted on 10 April 2014

963    ISO:

964    • ISO/TS 25237:2008(E) Health Informatics — Pseudonymization. Geneva, Switzerland.
965    2008. This ISO Technical Specification describes how privacy sensitive information can
966    be de-identified using a "pseudonymization service" that replaces direct identifiers with
967    pseudonyms. It is provides a set of terms and definitions that are considered authoritative
968    for this document.

969    UK:

970    • UK Anonymisation Network, http://ukanon.net/
971    • Anonymisation: Managing data protection risk, Code of Practice 2012, Information
972    Commissioner's Office. https://ico.org.uk/media/for-
973    organisations/documents/1061/anonymisation-code.pdf. 108 pages

974    US:

975    • McCallister, Erika, Tim Grance and Karen Scarfone, *Guide to Protecting the*
976    *Confidentiality of Personally Identifiable Information (PII)*, Special Publication 800-122,
977    National Institute of Standards and Technology, US Department of Commerce. 2010.
978    • US Department of Health & Human Services, Office for Civil Rights, Guidance
979    Regarding Methods for De-identification of Protected Health Information in Accordance
980    with the Health Insurance Portability and Accountability Act (HIPAA) Privacy Rule,
981    2010.
982    • Data De-identification: An Overview of Basic Terms, Privacy Technical Assistance
983    Center, US Department of Education. May 2013.
984    http://ptac.ed.gov/sites/default/files/data_deidentification_terms.pdf

985      • Statistical Policy Working Paper 22 (Second version, 2005), Report on Statistical
986        Disclosure Limitation Methodology, Federal Committee on Statistical Methodology,
987        December 2005.

988   **B.2   Law Review Articles and White Papers:**

989      • Barth-Jones, Daniel C., The 'Re-Identification' of Governor William Weld's Medical
990        Information: A Critical Re-Examination of Health Data Identification Risks and Privacy
991        Protections, Then and Now (June 4, 2012). Available at SSRN:
992        http://ssrn.com/abstract=2076397 or http://dx.doi.org/10.2139/ssrn.2076397
993      • Cavoukian, Ann, and El Emam, Khaled, De-identification Protocols: Essential for
994        Protecting Privacy, Privacy by Design, June 25, 2014.
995        https://www.privacybydesign.ca/content/uploads/2014/06/pbd-de-
996        identifcation_essential.pdf
997      • Lagos, Yianni, and Jules Polonetsky, Public vs. Nonpublic Data: the Benefits of
998        Administrative Controls, Stanford Law Review Online, 66:103, Sept. 3, 2013
999      • Ohm, Paul, Broken Promises of Privacy: Responding to the Surprising Failure of
1000      Anonymization (August 13, 2009). UCLA Law Review, Vol. 57, p. 1701, 2010; U of
1001      Colorado Law Legal Studies Research Paper No. 9-12. Available at SSRN:
1002      http://ssrn.com/abstract=1450006
1003     • Wu, Felix T. Defining Privacy and Utility in Data Sets, University of Colorado Law
1004      Review 84:1117 (2013).

1005   **B.3   Reports and Books:**

1006     • Committee on Strategies for Responsible Sharing of Clinical Trial Data, Board on Health
1007      Sciences Policy, *Sharing Clinical Trial Data: Maximizing Benefits, Minimizing Risk*,
1008      Institute of Medicine of the National Academies, The National Academies Press,
1009      Washington, DC. 2015.
1010     • Emam, Khaled El and Luk Arbuckle, *Anonymizing Health Data,* O'Reilly, Cambridge,
1011      MA. 2013

1012   **B.4   Survey Articles**

1013     • Chris Clifton and Tamir Tassa. 2013. On Syntactic Anonymity and Differential
1014      Privacy. *Trans. Data Privacy* 6, 2 (August 2013), 161-183.
1015     • Benjamin C. M. Fung, Ke Wang, Rui Chen and  Philip S. Yu, Privacy-Preserving Data
1016      Publishing: A Survey on Recent Developments, Computing Surveys, June 2010.
1017     • Ebaa Fayyoumi and B. John Oommen. 2010. A survey on statistical disclosure control
1018      and micro-aggregation techniques for secure statistical databases. *Softw. Pract.*
1019      *Exper.* 40, 12 (November 2010), 1161-1188. DOI=10.1002/spe.v40:12
1020      http://dx.doi.org/10.1002/spe.v40:12
1021     • Fayyoumi, E. and Oommen, B. J. (2010), A survey on statistical disclosure control and
1022      micro-aggregation techniques for secure statistical databases. Softw: Pract. Exper.,
1023      40: 1161–1188. doi: 10.1002/spe.992